JUDGE JUDY SHEINDLIN'S

Win or Lose by How You Choose!

JUDGE JUDY SHEINDLIN'S
Win or Lose by How You Choose!

ILLUSTRATED BY BOB TORE

Cliff Street Books
An Imprint of HarperCollins*Publishers*
www.harpercollins.com

Judge Judy Sheindlin's Win or Lose by How You Choose!
Copyright © 2000 by Judge Judy Sheindlin Illustrations copyright © 2000 by Bob Tore
All rights reserved. No part of this book may be used or reproduced in any manner whatsoever
without written permission except in the case of brief quotations embodied in critical articles and reviews.
Printed in the United States of America. For information address HarperCollins Children's Books,
a division of HarperCollins Publishers, 1350 Avenue of the Americas, New York, NY 10019
www.harperchildrens.com

Library of Congress Cataloging-in-Publication Data
Sheindlin, Judy, 1942–
    [Win or lose by how you choose!]
    Judge Judy Sheindlin's Win or lose by how you choose! / illustrated by Bob Tore.
        p.   cm.
    Summary: Multiple-choice questions about the right thing to do in different situations.
    ISBN 0-06-028780-2. — ISBN 0-06-028474-9 (lib. bdg.)
    1. Children—Conduct of life—Examinatons, questions, etc.—Juvenile literature.   [1. Conduct of life.]
I. Tore, Bob, ill.   II. Title.
BJ1631 .S44   2000
170—dc21   99-47109

2   3   4   5   6   7   8   9   10   ❖

This book is dedicated to our children—

Rachel, Danny, Joseph, Gregory, Jamie, Jonathan, Adam, and Nicole—

and to our grandchildren,

Casey, Taylor, Jenna, Sarah, baby Jake, and baby Abraham.

To Parents:

Where do children learn to be good people? Who teaches a child honesty, kindness, fairness, and loyalty? As parents, you have the unique opportunity to fashion the characters of your kids, and this book will be a useful tool. In this book I ask children questions about situations they face every day. With each question, I give them a series of answers to choose from, but I don't tell them the right answer. This way you, the parents, can explore and evaluate the different choices together with your child. I encourage you to use this book in your ongoing dialog with your children to teach them that the choices they make will determine the adults they will become.

To Kids:

You are beginning what I like to call the adventure of life. How you choose to live your life will make you a happy—or unhappy—adult. You will always be faced with choices . . . dozens every day. I hope this book will make you think of how to make the right choices to be a happy person and to have a happy life.

Judy Sheindlin

You just got your ice cream from the ice-cream man,
but he was so busy that he forgot to take your money.

You should:

A. Put the money back in your pocket and eat your ice cream.

B. Get his attention and tell him that you didn't pay yet.

C. Eat your ice cream fast and tell him you never got it.

D. Tell him you gave him a five-dollar bill and you didn't get any change.

You borrowed your friend's bike and accidentally broke it.

You should:

A. Tell her you had an accident and you will pay to have her bike fixed.

B. Tell her you didn't realize that her bike was broken.

C. Blame it on one of your other friends.

D. Try to convince her that her bike was broken when she lent it to you.

You're sitting in a doctor's waiting room reading a magazine. There's something in the magazine that you would like to tear out.

You should:

A. Remember what magazine you're reading and buy it yourself.

B. Ask the receptionist if you can tear it out.

C. Not ask and just tear it out.

D. Not tear it out and take the whole magazine.

The person in front of you at the store checkout walked away and left some items.

You should:

A. Mind your own business and just leave them there.

B. Tell the cashier that someone left her items.

C. Call her back and tell her she forgot some items.

D. Throw the items in one of your bags since they've already been paid for.

You pick up the phone and accidentally hear your sister talking to her boyfriend.

You should:

A. Hang up the phone.

B. Say hello as if you thought the call was for you.

C. Just listen. Very quietly.

D. Hum into the phone until it gets on their nerves.

All your friends are smoking. They are making fun of you because you are not.

You should:

A. Not listen to them and forget about smoking.

B. Make believe you smoke so that they stop bothering you.

C. Ask one of them for a cigarette.

D. Go buy a pack of cigarettes to be one of the guys.

You notice that the desk next to you, where your good friend sits, has been empty for three days.

You should:

A. Ask your teacher where she is.

B. Call her on the phone and ask her where she's been.

C. Not bother calling because it's too much trouble.

D. Go through her desk to see if there's anything in there that you can use.

You were visiting your friend and your dog had an accident on the floor in his living room.

You should:

A. Clean it up and apologize.

B. Tell your friend about it.

C. Move a chair over it so that it can't be seen.

D. Take your dog and leave without saying anything.

You're standing in line at the store checkout and
you see it's going to be a long wait.

You should:

A. Be patient and wait your turn.

B. Leave with your item and come back later to pay for it.

C. Take your item and leave without ever paying.

D. Cut to the front of the line and act like you were there first.

You are home alone and someone knocks on the door.

You should:

A. Not answer the door.

B. Ask who it is and open the door only if you know him or her.

C. Tell the person to come back when an adult is home.

D. Open the door.

An elderly woman is trying to get in the elevator
and she's carrying a lot of packages.

You should:

A. Ask if you can help her with the packages.

B. Just hold the door for her.

C. Rush into the elevator and press the close button so she
won't slow you down.

D. Get in first and if she makes it . . . she makes it!

Your friend loaned you a dollar and now he wants you to pay him back.

You should:

A. Put off paying him as long as possible.

B. Pay him the money that you owe him.

C. Tell him that another friend owes you a dollar so he should get the money from her.

D. Tell him that you don't remember borrowing any money.

You arrive at your friend's birthday party and realize that you forgot to bring a present.

You should:

A. Tell your friend that you are embarrassed and you will be sending her a gift.

B. Tell her you brought a present but it got lost in her house.

C. Sign your name on somebody else's present.

D. Eat as much as you can and sneak out early.

You're sitting at the lunch counter having a soda.
The person next to you finishes eating, leaves a big
tip, and walks away.

You should:

A. Keep drinking your soda and forget about the tip.

B. Tell the waitress that the man left her some money.

C. Slide the money over to your side when nobody is looking, so it will look as if you left the tip.

D. Take the money and use it to pay for your soda.

You're dying to have another piece of cake and your friend is so busy dancing that she's not eating hers.

You should:

A. Keep your hands off of it. She'll be right back.

B. Ask the waiter to bring you another piece.

C. Take a small piece; she'll never know the difference.

D. Eat the whole thing and tell her the waiter took it.

Your room is a mess and really has to be cleaned up.

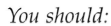

You should:

A. Start cleaning it up a little at a time.

B. Spend an entire day cleaning up your room.

C. Put it off to do some other day.

D. Forget about it. Your mother will take care of it.

You father left his car keys in the ignition.

You should:

A. Tell your father about the keys right away.

B. Take the keys out of the ignition and give them to your father.

C. Turn on the motor just to see what it feels like.

D. Drive the car around the block a couple of times.

A boy in your class just walked out of the bathroom with his fly opened.

You should:

A. Go over and whisper in his ear so that he knows.

B. Yell to him across the room that his fly is open.

C. Introduce him to some girls who are walking by.

D. Suggest that now would be a good time to get up in front of the class and speak.

You're picking up the mail and see that your brother received a letter marked "personal."

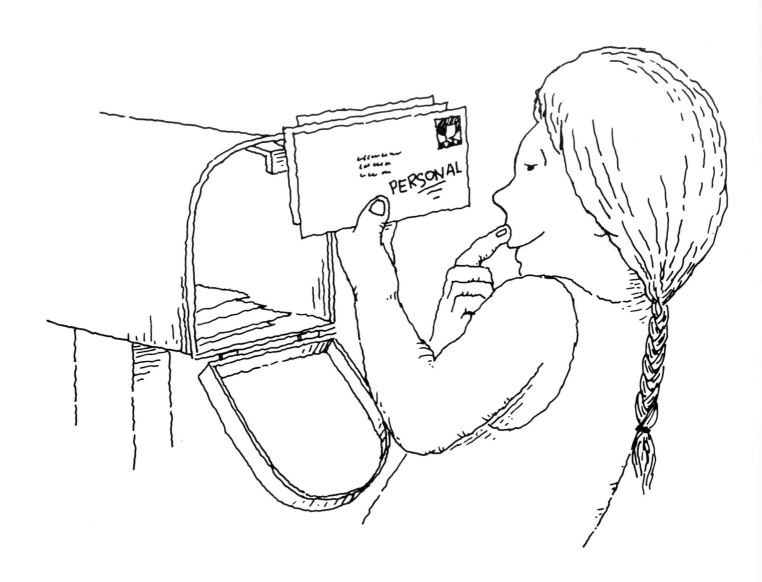

You should:

A. Give the letter to your brother.

B. Hold it up to the light to see what it says.

C. Open it up and read it.

D. Bring the letter to the park and read it to your friends.

You find a handgun in your father's closet.

You should:

A. Not touch it ever because it is off limits.

B. Ask your father to show it to you.

C. Pick it up to see how heavy it is.

D. Borrow it to show to your friends.

Your friend wants you to give him your homework.

You should:

A. Not give it to him and tell him why he should do it himself.

B. Offer to help him get his done.

C. Let him look at it for a few minutes and then take it back.

D. Give it to him because he is really a good friend and would do the same for you.

You didn't wipe your shoes when you came in and you tracked mud all over the carpet.

You should:

A. Clean it up.

B. Tell your mother what you did and ask her to help you clean it up.

C. Not say anything about it.

D. Yell out, "Hey! Look what somebody did!"

Mom always lets you have an extra lamb chop.
Tonight your sister invited her friend for dinner.

You should:

A. Start screaming that the extra lamb chop is yours and it's
   not right that your sister invited a friend.

B. Distract everybody and when no one is looking, take your
   father's lamb chop.

C. Forget about it and try to make her feel at home.

D. Sneak into the kitchen and eat the lamb chop before dinner
   is on the table.

Your neighbors are complaining that your TV is
very loud and it is keeping them up.

You should:

A. Tell them you don't know what they are talking about.

B. Apologize and lower the volume so that they can sleep.

C. Not pay any attention to them.

D. Make it louder because your neighbors are screaming and
you can't hear the TV.

A fight breaks out at school.

You should:

A. Round up all your friends and tell them something exciting is going on.

B. Tell a teacher as soon as you can.

C. Enjoy watching the fight and feel good that you aren't involved.

D. Take bets.

Your friend offers you a ride to the game in his old smelly car. You would rather go in your father's brand-new fancy car.

You should:

A. Tell your friend you promised your father you would go with him.

B. Ask your friend if he would like to come with you in your father's car.

C. Tell your friend that you get carsick when you ride in old cars.

D. Tell your friend you wouldn't be caught dead in his car.

The test answer sheet falls out of your teacher's bag.

You should:

A. Tell the teacher that she dropped it.

B. Ignore what you saw and just walk away.

C. Pick it up and read it.

D. Pick it up and share the answers with your friends.

Some birds have built a nest in the tree in front of your house. Your two friends are throwing rocks at the nest.

You should:

A. Run outside and start throwing rocks back at them.

B. Tell them to stop what they are doing because they are going to hurt the birds.

C. Threaten to go call their parents.

D. Run outside and climb up the tree to see if you can protect the birds.

You're playing basketball with some kids. Your friend accidentally wets his pants and wants to run home. He asks you not to tell anyone, but when he leaves, the team captain wants to know where he went.

You should:

A. Tell the captain as loud as you can, to make sure that everybody hears, that your friend wet his pants.

B. Tell your friend that you won't help him out and laugh at him.

C. Tell the captain that he had a personal problem and he will be right back.

D. Tell the captain you have no idea where he went.

Your friends begin to make fun of your new neighbor because she has big ears.

You should:

A. Walk away from your friends and say nothing.

B. Tell them to stop because it is unkind.

C. Suggest to your new neighbor that she wear a hat to cover her ears.

D. Make fun of her too.

Your best friend tells you a secret: Someone gave him
a drug to try.

You should:

A. Insist that he tell his parents.

B. Tell him to throw it away and that both of you should stay
   away from the person who gave him the drug.

C. Tell him that a lot of kids are using this stuff so there might
   be something to it.

D. Tell him it couldn't hurt to try it just once.

You are late to class.

You should:

A. Tell your teacher that you forgot today was a school day.

B. Cut class because you're late anyway.

C. Forge an excuse note from your parents.

D. Apologize to your teacher and promise to be on time in the future.

You promised your mother you would do your homework, but your friends are waiting for you to come out and play ball.

You should:

A. Sneak out the window—nobody will know.

B. Nag your mother until she lets you out just to get rid of you.

C. Rush through your homework so that you can go out.

D. Tell your friends you can't go.

You accidentally throw a ball through the classroom window.

You should:

A. Tell the teacher that you have no idea how it happened.

B. Demand a cash payment for damage to your ball.

C. Tell the teacher that you were responsible.

D. Blame it on the nearest little kid.

It's your dad's birthday and the family is going out for dinner—but your favorite program is on.

You should:

A. Try to get them to wait.

B. Tape it so that you can watch it later and go cheerfully to dinner.

C. Ask your mother if she can bring you back something to eat.

D. Go to dinner, but sulk through the whole meal.

Your classmate is copying from your paper during a test in school.

You should:

A. Cover your paper.

B. Tell him to stop.

C. Tell the teacher.

D. Let him copy from you because he can't pass the test otherwise.